GOD MAKES A PROMISE

FAITH-BUILDING STORIES

FOR KIDS

Also by Cari J. Haus:

Learning to Walk With God, with Dwight Hall

To order, call 1-800-765-6955.

Visit us at **www.reviewandherald.com**
for information on other Review and Herald® products.

REVIEW AND HERALD® PUBLISHING ASSOCIATION
HAGERSTOWN, MD 21741-1119

The author assumes full responsibility for the accuracy of all facts and quotations as cited in this book.

Unless otherwise noted, texts are from the *Holy Bible, New International Version.* Copyright © 1973, 1978, 1984, International Bible Society. Used by permission of Zondervan Bible Publishers.

This book was
Edited by Gerald Wheeler
Cover design by Tina Ivany
Cover art by Raoul Vitale
Interior design by Candy Harvey
Electronic makeup by Shirley M. Bolivar
Typeset: 11/13 Cheltenham

PRINTED IN U.S.A.

10 09 08 07 06 5 4 3 2 1

R&H Cataloging Service
Haus, Cari J., 1960- .
Faith-building stories for kids. Book 2. God makes a promise.

1. Bible stories. I. Title.

220.9505

ISBN 978-0-8280-1893-7

Contents

CHAPTER • 1

The Very First Baby

"*Waah! Waah!*" A new sound spread across Planet Earth, and all the nearby animals stopped to listen. Perhaps Adam's pet kitten peeked from behind his legs. Maybe a playful puppy bounced over to see what was going on. We can be sure the angels were watching, and with very good reason. For though colts and calves and a hundred other types of animal babies had already been born, this was the first human baby.

We don't know how large Cain was when he first entered the world, but he must have been a big baby. And what lungs he must have had! No doubt he made good use of them, too.

Like most

parents, Adam and Eve must have found Baby Cain to be incredibly interesting. How tenderly they must have held him, cooed to him, and whispered in his ear. They must have been excited when the child started to smile, wave his chubby arms, and then walk and talk for the very first time. It must have comforted them to know that, even in the middle of the death and decay caused by sin, there would still be life—vibrant new life on our planet.

Because Cain was their very first son, Adam and Eve had especially high hopes for him. They even wished he could be their promised deliverer—the one to save them from their sins. But unfortunately, this was not to be the case. It would be many more years before Jesus came as a baby to our world.

As the boy grew older, Adam and Eve told him stories just as other parents would do in the years to come. Of course, it meant that they had to share with him one of the saddest stories of all—how they gave up paradise for a piece of fruit and had to leave the Garden of Eden because of their sin.

Then Adam and Eve took Cain to the gate of the beautiful Garden of Eden. Though a mighty angel with a flaming sword now blocked the gate, the first family could still look inside.

Adam stared sadly at the garden as he held Cain in his arms.

"This is where we could have lived, if we hadn't sinned," he told his son.

Cain held the baby lamb they had brought along as Adam began to pile up stones for an altar.

"What are we going to do, Father?" the boy wanted to know. A lump rose in Adam's throat as he

looked down at his little son. He knew how hard it was for God to give up Jesus, and he also knew it would be hard for Cain to give up that little lamb.

"My son," Adam's voice broke, "we must sacrifice this lamb. God has told us to do this, because it will help us understand how terrible sin really is."

"But this lamb didn't do anything," Cain protested.

"Yes," Adam replied. "He is innocent—just like Jesus, the innocent lamb of God. But he will pay the price just the same."

No doubt Cain and Adam both cried when they sacrificed that lamb. But God was trying to teach them an important lesson—one that Adam would also need to teach Cain's younger brothers and sisters as they grew from children to adults. Their father wanted them to love the good and hate the evil. To stay close to God and shrink from sin.

It was Adam and Eve's job, as the first earthly parents, to plant seeds of goodness in their children's hearts. To tell their offspring about God and Satan. Then the children were to tend and water these seeds of goodness as their own love for God grew stronger and stronger in their hearts.

Of course, Adam and Eve did everything they could to help water and grow those seeds of goodness, too. But like their parents before them, each child would have decisions to make. They could choose to be sorry for their sins and to love and obey God. Or they could question God and be angry with Him, just as Lucifer had first done in heaven.

Sorry to say, the very first child to be born on earth chose to water the weeds of evil in his heart. He let himself feel angry with God, perhaps from a very young age. Although he didn't show it on the outside, at least not at first, those plants of selfishness, anger, and doubt grew stronger and stronger with each passing day. Cain didn't understand where he was going just then, but he was headed for a pile of trouble. Trouble that would cause a great deal of sadness not only for himself, but for his parents, family, and the entire world.

CHAPTER • 2

So Alike—Yet So Different

It's hard to imagine how two brothers could be so alike in so many ways—yet so different—as Cain and Abel. The very first boys on this planet and the sons of Adam and Eve, they lived in a beautiful land near the Garden of Eden. They sang the same songs as they grew up, heard the same stories, and were raised to love and obey the same God.

But unfortunately, this is where the similarity stopped. For though Cain and Abel had many things in common on the outside and may have even looked alike, the thoughts of their hearts couldn't have been more different.

Abel loved

God and was loyal to Him. He understood that the Lord was fair and good. And he was thankful that Jesus would come and die for him so that he could not only live, but someday move to the beautiful Garden of Eden he had heard so much about.

Cain, on the other hand, thought that God had been too hard on Adam and Eve in punishing them for sin. Unfortunately, Cain let his mind keep questioning God until he felt very bitter.

When Satan tempted Eve in the Garden of Eden, it was a test that God allowed to see if the first human beings would be loyal to Him. God also had a test for Cain and Abel. He loved them, and wanted to know if they would love Him in return.

God's test for the two brothers had something to do with their offerings to Him. You see, right from the very beginning God had told Adam, Eve, and their boys how Jesus would have to die on the cross someday. Cain and Abel understood that Jesus was as innocent as a lamb. They understood that the lamb represented Jesus and all that He would do for them. They also knew that it was only through Jesus, the "Lamb of God," that they could be rescued from their sins and live an obedient life.

As young boys, Cain and Abel had watched their father Adam offer lambs for his sins and the sins of his family many times. But now they had grown into young men, and it was time for them to offer a lamb for themselves. God had loved them and cared for them all their lives, and now, through the sacrifice they would make, He wanted to see if they would accept and return His love. Only one question now needed to be settled: Would both brothers pass the test?

CHAPTER • 3

One "A" and One "F"

It was a busy day for Cain and Abel when they built their first altars. They had a place to choose, rocks to find, and last but not least—the sacrifice to get ready.

"Come, little lamb." Abel stood by the gate of his sheepfold. He had picked his prize sheep to give on this special day. As he carried it to the altar he stroked the lamb's head.

"God is giving His son to die for me," he whispered in the lamb's ear. "I must give my best as well."

Sadly Abel laid the little lamb on the altar. After running a hand gently over its face for the very last time, Abel raised a knife and took the animal's life.

"Please forgive my sins," he said as he knelt by the altar, his head bowed in grief. "Help me not to make the same mistakes again. Help me to understand that when I sin, I hurt Jesus just as I hurt this sweet lamb."

Raising his head slowly, Abel opened his eyes, almost afraid to look at the altar. There was only one question in his heart now: would God accept his gift?

Whoosh! A stream of fire swept down from heaven, burning up the little lamb, the wood beneath it, and even the stones on the altar.

Abel smiled, and up in heaven God was smiling too. Not because a lamb had died, for that made them both very sad. The young man was happy because he had peace in his heart. He truly loved God and knew his sins were forgiven. As for God, He looked past the sacrifice, right into Abel's heart. God saw that Adam's son was sorry for his sins. That he understood it would be hard for God to give up His Son to die—harder than giving up his prize lamb. God had a friend in Abel, and because God loves to have us humans as His friends, He was happy too.

Not far from Abel's altar, big brother Cain was busily finishing one of his own. Like Abel, Cain was hoping for fire from heaven. But there was a problem with his offering, however. Cain had brought fruit from his garden instead of a lamb! It was nice fruit, to be sure, but it wasn't what God wanted as an offering.

This might seem like a small thing, but it wasn't. Cain knew a lamb stood for Jesus, but he didn't want to do things God's way. He didn't think that he needed Jesus, the Lamb of God, to die for his sins.

Instead, He thought his own fruits or good deeds should be enough!

Although God loved him very much, Cain's offering wasn't acceptable at all. He needed Jesus, the Lamb of God. Jesus was, and still is, the only way to heaven. Good deeds, though important, could never pay for a ticket to heaven.

Then God looked into Cain's heart. He saw anger and selfishness lurking inside. Worse yet, Cain wasn't really sorry for his sins.

Unfortunately, Cain and Abel are like two kinds of people still alive in the world today. As did Abel, some people understand that Jesus died for their sins. They know they can't make it to heaven by themselves, so they trust in Him to save them. Others think they can get to heaven by their own good deeds. They need Jesus just as badly as anyone else, but they don't think they do. And then, because their sins are not covered by the "blood of the lamb," they can't be accepted in heaven.

Nearly every false religion in the world teaches, in some way or other, that people can save themselves. Some even claim that a person can get better and better without Jesus' help. Following Cain's example, they want to reach heaven through their own good deeds.

Through the sad story of Cain we can learn what happens when we try to get to heaven by ourselves. Because we have fallen into sin, we humans can't possibly make ourselves better. In fact, when human beings try to "do it on their own," things just get worse. They go down instead of up!

Jesus is our only hope to be saved, for the Bible declares that there is no other name under heaven by which we may be saved, and that there is no salvation in any other person (Acts 4:12).

The Bible also tells us that those who truly love God will obey Him. And they will obey all His commandments—not just the ones they like or agree with.

When Cain brought an offering to the altar, he obeyed one of God's commands. But when it was an offering that stood for his own good deeds, he disobeyed another of God's commandments.

Since the time sin began there have always been people who, like Cain, obey only some of God's commandments. They want His blessing and approval, even though they don't do what He asks them to do!

But the Bible tells us that faith without obedience ("works") is "dead" (James 2:17). In other words, if we really believe God, our lives will change from the inside out. But if our faith isn't strong enough to affect our lives, it's really not faith at all. Worse than that, the Bible warns that those who say they know God but don't obey His commandments are liars, that the truth is not in them (1 John 2:4)!

Unfortunately, that's exactly what was happening to Cain.

CHAPTER • 4

The Not-so-mysterious Murder

Cain was already angry when he first brought his fruit to the altar, but he got really mad when no fire came. As an older brother, he was especially irritated that God whooshed fire on Abel's altar and not his own.

"Don't you like fruit?" He glared toward the Garden of Eden. His whole attitude, the look on his face, and the anger in his eyes were so different than his brother's that even the animals must have noticed.

Now God loved Cain. The young man was His child. And God wanted him to understand what was really happening. So He had a talk with His wayward son.

"Why are you so upset?" God's voice

boomed out of the garden. "If you do what's right, the fire will come. But if you do wrong, look out! Sin is waiting for you—right outside your door."

His hour of decision had come. Cain had a choice to make. He could accept the sacrifice of Jesus for his sins or keep doing things his own way. Either he could choose to love Jesus or keep on complaining.

Unfortunately, Cain continued to make wrong decisions. And as his anger grew against God, it also became hotter against his brother. He stalked across the field to where Abel was still kneeling.

"You must think you're pretty special, getting fire down from heaven and all that," the older brother shouted. Abel looked up at him. His face was so happy, so peaceful, that it made Cain madder than ever.

"I'm not better than anyone else," Abel replied quietly. "I just did what God asked me to do." His eyes looked pleadingly at his brother. "You can do that too, Cain."

"God isn't fair," Cain sulked. "He shouldn't have thrown our parents out of the garden."

"God is fair," Abel said gently. "He could have let our parents die right away. But He let them live, so they could learn to love Him for what He really is."

Abel's eyes rested on the face of his older brother. It seemed so strange to be disagreeing with Cain. All their lives he had been the leader. Whether they were climbing trees, skipping stones, or hopscotching across a brook, Cain led and Abel followed. Like most younger boys, Abel loved to follow the oldest. But when his brother chose to rebel against God, Abel knew he had to stop. He drew a line right there and refused to cross it. More than that, he wanted to win his brother back to God.

"Jesus loves you," he told him. "He's going to die for us someday. That's what the lamb is all about." Abel stood, shifting from one foot to another. He had never seen Cain so angry—yet he had to go on.

"Why don't you bring God a lamb?" he pleaded. "God will send fire if you'll bring the lamb."

Cain's eyes narrowed. His face grew redder than ever. Then he flew into a full-blown, out of control temper-tantrum. He couldn't sling meteors like Satan, but the spirit of Satan—the spirit of hate and rebellion—was raging in his heart.

"Well," he thundered, "who do you think you are, telling me how to please God?"

Then Cain struck Abel. Whether he had something in his hand or not, the Bible doesn't say. But it's very clear that Cain killed his brother.

Cain couldn't stand to be around Abel because his brother was doing what was right. Abel's character reminded him of his own sin, and he couldn't stand it.

In the years since that first terrible murder many others have followed Cain's example. God's disobedient children hate the ones who are doing right. The Christian lives of those who love and obey Jesus show up the sins in their own hearts, and they can't stand it. "Everyone who does evil hates the light, and will not come into the light for fear that his deeds will be exposed" (John 3:20).

The stronger the light shining from the Christian's life, the darker the hate from those choosing not to follow Jesus. Because their sins are seen more clearly in the light shining near them, they snuff out the candles that disturb their peace.

In the Garden of Eden God told Adam and Eve that sin would cause a war between not only Satan and God, but the followers of each. That's what the Lord meant when He said to Satan that He would put "enmity between you and the woman, and between your offspring and hers" (Genesis 3:15).

The murder of Abel was the first of many bad things yet to happen in the long and bitter war between the good and the bad. When Satan sees people like Abel, people choosing to love and obey God, it makes him very angry. He wants everybody to believe it's impossible to obey God's law, but those who truly love God show by their holy actions how wrong he really is.

So Satan stirs up his followers to hurt the ones who love God. He's done it all through history, and he's still doing it today. During the centuries-long battle between good and evil Satan and his followers have killed many good people. Often called martyrs, they have lost their lives for Jesus' sake. But they have won the battle with Satan. Abel was the very first martyr. He lost his life for doing right, but someday soon he'll live again in heaven.

CHAPTER • 5

Doubling the Curse

I can't believe he would do that!" Abel's guardian angel had just flown in with the terrible news, and all heaven reeled with the shock of the murder. Gloomy faces filled the once-happy courts. Angels who'd known nothing but joy had now seen a war in heaven, a fight for the earth, and now on top of all that, a murder.

If Cain thought no one saw what he did, he didn't know God very well. For the Lord sees everything everywhere in the entire universe, and His angels are watching too.

Of course, God still loved Cain in spite of his wicked action. He loved Cain so much, in fact, that He gave him a chance to confess or even say he was sorry. But God didn't point a finger at Cain. Instead,

He just asked a question.

"Where is your brother?" the Lord wanted to know.

"I have no idea," Cain fired back. "Am I his babysitter?"

Poor Cain! Somehow he'd forgotten that God, who was always with him, knew all he said or did. He even thought he could lie to God! As for God, He could see that Cain wasn't sorry for what he had done. He'd allowed Cain time to think about the murder and even given him a chance to say he was sorry. But now it was time for Cain to receive something else—his punishment.

"What have you done?" God asked sternly. "I know you killed your brother. And now here is your punishment: When you plant a pear tree, it won't give you as much fruit as before. It'll be that way with your whole garden. You'll have to work extra hard, just to make things grow. Even worse, you'll spend the rest of your life running from others, always afraid someone will take revenge for what you did to your brother."

The Lord had already put one curse on the earth at the time of the very first sin. As a result, it was already harder to grow things. But now, because of Cain's terrible sin, God doubled the terrible curse. Of course, this wasn't the way God had hoped things would happen. But by keeping people busy with more work, He was giving them less time to get into trouble.

God could have ended Cain's life right then. But He didn't. In His great love, God still hoped that this very first child to be born on earth would someday realize what he had done, or even be sorry for his sin.

But sorry to say, Cain only became more of a

rebel. Shaking his fist at God, the Garden of Eden, and even his parents, he packed up his family and moved away. Worse yet, he became bolder and bolder in his hatred toward God. In fact, he was one of the sinful leaders that led God to wash this world with a flood.

Cain's life is a sad example of what happens when people give themselves up to sin. Their behavior gets worse and worse until the day they die. In Cain's time the wicked had nearly a thousand years to sin in. No doubt this is why, in time, God decided to shorten the lifespan of human beings down to about 120 years. One hundred and twenty years would be long enough for people to choose who they would love and obey. In the meantime, those who rebelled against God wouldn't be around for such a long time to sin and influence others.

One can only imagine how much Satan gloated over the very first murder. Getting Cain to hate God was part of his wicked plan—a plan he's still working hard at today. Satan is very organized and powerful, and he wants to trick you as he did Cain. More than ever, he wants you to hate God as he does.

Fortunately, God is more powerful than Satan. He knows everything that has happened, will happen, and should happen in our world. In fact, He has a very detailed plan for the Earth. Stopping Satan's rebellion is only a part of His wonderful plan. He also wants to show the entire universe—including human beings—what the rebellion is all about.

God didn't want Cain to kill Abel, but He used that sad situation to let everyone know that He is both loving and fair.

"I can't believe he would do that!" were the words

not only of the angels who saw Cain kill Abel, but beings from other planets. God's other created beings were also watching, with the angels, the sad events on Planet Earth. In the murder of Abel, the sadness of Adam and Eve at the loss of their second son, and the many sins that followed that horrible day, they saw how evil humans became, and how their thoughts were constantly wicked. People fought each other, sinking deeper and deeper into the miry pit of sin. Thus the beings of other worlds learned what would happen when Satan was in charge.

The story of this world—and the war between Christ and Satan for it—has been unfolding since the days of Adam and Eve, Cain and Abel, and their descendants. And through that story, God is trying to tell us something very wonderful about Himself. It is history, His-story. And in the end, His story and the record of the love and care with which He handled this world will show once and for all that He is kind, loving, and true. Someday, rebels such as Lucifer and Cain will be no more. There will be no more rebellion in that day, for everyone will know that it leads only to death. And in that great day when Satan is judged, the entire universe will not only understand God, but say all together: "just and true are your ways, King of the ages" (Revelation 15:3).

CHAPTER • 6

Just Like His Daddy

Of course, we can only imagine how terrible Adam and Eve felt about all of this. In one day they lost Abel, whom no doubt had been the pride and joy of their heart, and Cain, whom they had so hoped would love, serve, and honor God.

After Abel died, God blessed Adam and Eve with another baby boy. They named him Seth, and, like Abel before him, he would receive a very special gift. It was the "spiritual birthright," and the person who had it was to teach his children about God. In addition, Seth was to be the great-great-very-great grandfather of Jesus Christ Himself.

Of course, Adam and Eve were very happy when Seth was born. They must have known that God had chosen him for something special, too, because that's what the name "Seth" means.

Eve smiled as she snuggled the tiny one in her arms.

"God gave me this boy in place of Abel, who Cain killed," she said.

As you might expect with parents as tall as Adam and Eve, Seth didn't stay tiny for long. In fact, he probably wasn't all that small when he was born. But he grew and just kept on growing until he was taller than Cain or Abel had ever been. Seth looked like his daddy too—at least, more than the other boys. But even more importantly, he acted like his father. In other words, Seth chose to love and honor God as Adam and Abel had done.

It doesn't mean Seth was a "goodie-goodie." Being good wasn't any more natural for Seth than it was for Cain. Adam had been made perfect—in the image of God. But Seth was born in a world of sin because of what his parents had done.

Adam and Eve taught him about Jesus and how He would die to save us someday. They wanted their son to be holy and good, and, through the grace of God, Seth made the right choice. He decided that he would love and serve God just as Abel would have if he were still alive. Seth wanted to help others learn how to love and obey God, too.

Abel had lived a simple life—like a shepherd in tents or booths—and the children of Seth lived the same way. These children of God thought of themselves as strangers and pilgrims in this world. Like their grandfather Adam, they were looking forward to life in a better world—that is, a heavenly one.

CHAPTER • 7

The Daughters of Men

The Bible doesn't tell us a lot about Seth, but we do know that he also had a son. His name was Enos. Unfortunately, by the time Enos was born people were more and more bold about their sinning. Because of this, those who served God began to call themselves the "sons of God." On the other hand, those who didn't love and obey God fell deeper and deeper into sin. In other words, they acted worse and worse. They even made fun of God and His holy law.

After God told Cain what his punishment would be for killing Abel, he moved away from the home of his parents. He was still a gardener, but now he also became a builder. Cain made his own city and named it after his oldest boy.

In time, Cain drifted farther and farther from God. He wanted to get all the pleasure he could out of life right now—every day. So he threw away the promise that someday, if faithful to God, he could live in the beautiful Garden of Eden.

Cain was a great leader, but, sorry to say, he led his children and all who would follow away from God. He and his followers worshiped Satan, the god of this world, rather than the God of heaven. They became rich and built many beautiful things. But they couldn't have cared less about God. Instead, they took their stand against His plan for human beings.

In the Garden of Eden God had given Adam and Eve the beautiful gift of the Sabbath. Even after they left Eden the first couple set aside that day as holy to worship and spend special time with Him. They and all their children who chose to serve God kept that day holy. But Cain and his children ignored the Sabbath. They chose their own time to work and their own time to rest. They didn't care what God said at the Garden of Eden, and they weren't afraid to show it by their lives.

For some time after Cain left his parents and built his own city, his children and those who served God lived separately. But as Cain's family continued to grow, his children began moving into the plains and valleys where the children of Seth dwelled.

Naturally, the children of Seth were concerned about the influence of people who didn't serve God. So the children of Seth moved to the mountains, where they could serve God as they pleased. As long as the children of Seth stayed away from the children of Cain, they chose to worship God with their whole heart. But little by little, through the years, they mixed with the children of Cain.

Unfortunately, this mingling of the followers of God with those who hated Him had a very bad result. The Bible says that "the sons of God saw that the daughters of men were beautiful" (Genesis 6:2). Seth's grandchildren and great-grandchildren began to marry the beautiful women of Cain's family. This disappointed God. Many of the people who had until then worshiped God now were tempted into sin by the things that were now all around them. As a result, they lost their unique and holy character or way of doing things. By spending lots of time with those who hated and dishonored God, they became like them in many ways.

The Bible tells us that a man should have one wife, and a wife should have one husband. But soon the children of Cain began to break this commandment. The men married as many wives as they wanted to. And sadly, the children of Seth became just like the children of Cain. They spent all their time thinking about the pleasures they could have and forgot about God's commandments.

They didn't like to keep God in their thoughts. In the words of the Bible, "their thinking became futile and their foolish hearts were darkened" (Romans 1:21). Because of this, the Bible says that God gave them over to a mind lacking judgment. This means they had made so many bad choices that they didn't know right from wrong anymore.

As a result, sin began to creep all over the earth. The disease of sin was affecting more and more of God's children.

CHAPTER • 8

A Very Sad Grandpa

Poor Great-grandfather Adam! He lived and saw many of his children acting worse and worse for nearly a thousand years. How he tried to stop this terrible tide of evil.

"Raise up your children in the way of the Lord," God had told Adam. And Adam did his best to do so. Carefully treasuring all the things God had taught him, he told them again and again to his children, grandchildren, and great-grandchildren.

"How happy I used to be, back in the Garden of Eden," he said to all who would listen. Then, painful as it was, he described how he had fallen into sin and all the terrible things that had happened because of that one horrible mistake.

"God wants you to keep His law," Adam went on. "Even the little things matter." Of course, he also explained to them all about the plan of salvation—how someday Jesus would die for the sins of the world.

But like many children in the world today, most of Grandfather Adam's offspring wouldn't listen. In fact, many of Adam's children and grandchildren weren't even nice to him. Some felt angry with Adam for his part in bringing sin into the world.

"This is all your fault, anyway," they hurled in his face. "So don't try telling us how to live."

Adam was a humble man, and sadness over what he had done now filled his life. When he had left the Garden of Eden, the very idea that he might die someday had horrified him. He had cried when the first falling leaf fluttered down from a tree! What tears he had shed over the first lamb sacrificed, and the many others that were to come. And how he had sobbed with Eve over the grave of their son Abel.

And now, as Adam neared the end of his life, he understood much more fully what death really meant. Perhaps he saw Eve's hair turn gray and, looking into the clear blue waters of a lake, discovered his face covered with wrinkles. But the very worst thing he had to watch was the leprosy of sin creeping over the world—a disease so bad that someday it could cause God to destroy the beautiful earth He had made. After watching the world fill with sorrow and sadness for 1,000 years, the sentence of death that God had given Adam didn't seem so bad after all.

He actually felt it was kind of the Lord to let him die so that he wouldn't have to watch what was happening to God's beautiful world anymore. And so

God Makes a Promise

Adam came to the end of a long and busy life. He had lived nearly 1,000 years and, in a world of sorrow and sin, that seemed plenty long enough.

CHAPTER • 9

The Age of Intelligence

Have you ever heard of cavemen? If so, you probably know what they're supposed to be like. "Wild" is the best word to describe the way people have pictured them, with their bushy hair, unruly beards, and clubs brandished high overhead as they stalked some overgrown beast.

Strangely enough, some people think this is what Adam's children were like. They believe that they were primitive, perhaps even stupid. That they had to "invent" fire, the wheel, and a lot of other simple things that we take for granted today. Of course, nothing could be farther from the truth. The Bible is clear that God created human beings in His image, and God is incredibly intelligent. So it stands to reason that Adam, Eve, and their children were pretty smart, too.

It's true that many of the people who lived before the flood were very wicked. But they certainly weren't cavemen, and, in spite of their wrong choices, they weren't stupid either! Instead, they had strong, healthy bodies and very powerful minds to go with them.

Some people assume that Adam's children might have taken longer to become teenagers, especially since they lived for centuries anyway. But that is another wrong idea. Except for being much bigger and smarter, teenagers back then were very much like teenagers now.

Of course, their parents were wiser too. In fact, the best and brightest people of our time couldn't hold a candle to these mental and physical giants of ages past. Today, the world honors scholars who spend 20 or 50 years learning about physics or science or math. But people before the flood had a real advantage. They could work on the same project for centuries! And it didn't hurt to have Adam for a teacher, either, for he was very wise. He had learned much in the Garden of Eden, right from the lips of God, and he shared his vast knowledge of science, religion, and other topics faithfully with his many children.

Eventually seven generations lived on this world all at the same time. They could talk to each other about what they knew, learn from each other, and pass all their knowledge around.

When we understand these things, it's easy to see that those early days of the world weren't an age of hairy cave people waving clubs like some people like to think. Instead, it was an age of great light. Everybody could learn from Adam. Those who loved and served God even had Jesus and the angels for their teachers. They also had a silent and very powerful lesson book right before their eyes, for the Garden of Eden was still with them, guarded by holy angels.

Even those who chose not to believe God couldn't say the Garden of Eden didn't exist, because they could see it with their own eyes. The whole world knew about the Garden of Eden, what had happened there, and why they couldn't go in.

Adam's children and grandchildren also understood that God was the ruler of all and that they were required to keep His holy law. In fact, it would have been hard not to know this while Adam was still alive.

Even though sin had spread through the earth, there was still a line of holy people who loved and worshiped God. People who spent so much time talking with and getting to know Him that a holy light shone from their faces. Though they lived in this world, their hearts were focused on heaven. They were the very first missionaries. Like all of God's people today, it was their job to live holy lives not only themselves, but to teach others how to live godly lives too. Like bright lamps shining in the darkness, they illumined the path toward heaven for their friends, children, and all who were yet to come.

CHAPTER • 10

God Finds a Friend

Although the Bible only mentions a few of God's followers who lived before the Flood, God has always had people who were faithful to Him.

One of God's followers was a man named Enoch. Enoch was part of a holy line of people—a people who kept alive the light of true faith even in sin's dark night. In fact, Enoch was one of the great-great-very-great grandfathers of Jesus Christ Himself.

Like so many of his brothers, sisters, cousins, and other relatives, he heard the sad story of how sin began right from the lips of Adam. He also learned from Adam how Jesus would die for his sins someday. Early in his life, Enoch made the decision to love and serve Jesus.

The Bible tells us that when Enoch was

65 years old he had a son. Now, Enoch had always loved God and tried to keep His commandments. But although he had loved God all his life, it wasn't until he and his wife had a baby boy that Enoch realized how much God really loved him, and how much he, in turn, should love.

"Hello little one!" he must have murmured as he held the child for the very first time. "I am your daddy, and I love you."

Enoch stroked the tiny boy's forehead thoughtfully as his wife looked on. A strange look came over his face.

"What is it, Enoch?" his wife wanted to know.

"Oh, I was just thinking about what it means to be a father, and how much I love Methusaleh. I am your daddy!" Enoch murmured to himself as he held the baby. As the years passed he was also touched by how much his little son loved and trusted him.

Through being a father, Enoch also realized how much more he should trust his own heavenly Father to care for his needs. He also began to realize how hard it must be for God to give up Jesus, His Son, to die for the sins of the world. Enoch thought about these things a lot, and as he did, he grew closer and closer to God.

Though Enoch loved God and thought about Him a lot, he didn't go off and live by himself. Instead, he showed God's love in all the little things of ordinary life to all those around him. Enoch was not a hermit. He had a work to do for God, and he knew it.

Whether he was with his family or other people, whether he was acting as a husband or a father, a friend or citizen of the place where he lived, Enoch

was a faithful, steadfast servant of God. His heart was in tune with God's heart. That means they made beautiful music together!

In one verse of the Bible God asks whether two people can walk together if they don't agree or think the same way. Well, God and Enoch were "agreed." And the Bible tells us that Enoch "walked with God," or stayed close and agreed with God, for 300 years!

Many Christians try to live closer to God if they think they are going to die soon, or that Jesus is coming soon. But Enoch didn't know how long it would be until Jesus would come. And yet he lived closer and closer to God as the decades and centuries rolled by.

Enoch was a very intelligent man, and he learned many things. But in addition to the things he learned from those around him, God gave him special knowledge from heaven. In other words, he was a prophet.

A very humble man, the closer he came to God, the more he realized how weak and imperfect he was. The growing wickedness in the world especially bothered him. In fact, he worried that the wickedness all around him would make him not reverence God as much.

And so Enoch tried to avoid spending a lot of time with those who dishonored God. Whenever he could, he went off by himself to talk with and think about God. Soon Enoch was breathing prayers almost as often as he breathed the air. And as he did, he lived in the very atmosphere of heaven. Though his body was still on earth, his heart was growing closer and closer to God.

CHAPTER • 11

Heaven in His Face

Whoosh! Enoch was right in the middle of a prayer one day when an angel swept out of heaven and stood by his side.

"Uh, hello!" Enoch must have said.

"Hello," the angel replied. "Were you hoping to get answers to some of your questions?"

"Why, yes," Enoch stammered. "There are a few things I just can't seem to understand."

"Look up." The angel rested his hand, ever so gently, on the man's shoulder. Enoch did as he was told, and as he did, God turned on His heavenly TV screen and flashed a vision of glory right before Enoch's eyes.

For some time Enoch had wondered what happens when a person dies.

Murders and accidents were happening all around him, and he didn't feel sure whether those who died would ever rise again. So God answered Enoch's question with a vision.

A picture of Jesus flashed up on the heavenly screen, and, looking into the future, Enoch saw him live and suffer and die.

"Hallelujah!" Enoch must have said when he saw Jesus rise from the grave. But wait! There was more! Saints of all colors, ages, and sizes came up with Him! The vision flashed from one scene to another, as Enoch saw the human race grow more and more wicked until the day God destroyed the world with a flood.

Enoch also saw how wicked the earth would be when Jesus came the second time. He saw a world full of stubborn, proud, and presumptuous people when Christ returned. They dishonored God and trampled on His law, not even caring that He had died for them. In his vision Enoch also witnessed those who loved God crowned with glory and honor while the wicked were punished, sent from the presence of God forever, and destroyed by a cleansing fire.

That day Enoch became a preacher of righteousness. He had seen the end of the world, the wonderful love of God, and the truth of divine judgment, and he couldn't help telling others about the incredible things he'd seen.

Those who loved and honored God loved to spend time with Enoch, to learn from this holy man and pray with him. But he didn't work only with them. He gave God's messages to all who would listen. Enoch even went to the land of Cain and preached God's message of salvation and judgment there.

"Behold!" he said solemnly. "For the Lord comes, with ten thousand of His saints. And He is going to bring judgment for everybody, and He will convince all who aren't godly of their ungodly deeds" (see Jude 14, 15).

Although Enoch loved the people, he wasn't afraid to speak against sin. While he longed to teach about the love of Jesus and begged the people to turn from their wicked ways, he also warned them that God would judge them for their deeds.

Though He often speaks words of love and compassion, God also sends messages that are sharp as a two-edged sword. Enoch sometimes had to say some hard things. Yet in spite of his difficult message, God's power was with him, and all the people knew it.

Some people even listened to the prophet's warning and put away their sins. But, sadly, most of the people laughed at his solemn warnings. In fact, they grew even bolder in their evil ways.

In the last days of our world's history God's people will bring a message to the world that is much like the teachings of Enoch. And as in the case of Enoch, many will respond to it with mockery and unbelief.

The people before the Flood rejected the warnings of Enoch, a holy man who walked with God. And, unfortunately, many people living today will do the same thing.

Enoch didn't let the rejection of the people bother him, though. Instead, he just spent more and more time with God. Somehow, even in the middle of his active and busy life, he always managed to have lots of time to talk with God. In fact, the busier he was, the more constant were his prayers. Enoch would stay with the people for a while, working to help them to go closer to God. Then He would go off by himself, hungering and thirsting for the knowledge that only God can give.

Spending a lot of time with God and talking with Him, Enoch became more and more like his Maker. His face shone with a holy light, the same light that shines in the face of Jesus. When Enoch came back from his quiet times with God, even the wicked were amazed. They saw something different about him, for the marks of heaven were on his happy face.

CHAPTER • 12

Pathway to Heaven

By now the world had become so wicked that God decided to destroy it. Of course, that was a big step for the Lord who had taken such delight in making His beautiful world. But it goes to show just how bad things had really become. The dark clouds of judgment hovered lower and lower over the earth.

During this difficult time Enoch remained faithful to the God he loved. He also pleaded and begged and worked to turn back the wickedness of the world and to put off God's judgment. Even though the sinful, pleasure-loving people wouldn't listen to him, he had the assurance that God approved of his efforts. And so he continued to battle faithfully against all the wickedness in the world.

"You're not very smart, Enoch" the people around him sneered. They couldn't understand why he wasn't trying to get rich. But his heart was on the treasures that last forever. In his visions he had looked into the celestial city. He had seen the King in His glory. And he was so in love with God that his heart, and even the things he said, were always in heaven.

The greater the sin around him, the more Enoch longed to go live with God. Even though his home was on earth, he lived by faith in the realms of light. The Bible says, "blessed are the pure in heart, for they will see God" (Matthew 5:8), Enoch had been walking in purity of heart for 300 years. For three centuries he walked with God. Every day he wanted to get closer and closer to God, and he did get closer and closer, until the day God took him home to Himself. Enoch stood on the doorstep of the eternal world, with only a step between him and heaven. And one very special day, the doors opened. Enoch walked right through the gates of heaven, the very first human being to enter there.

Back on earth people greatly missed him. His voice, which they had heard day after day in teaching and warning, was now silent. The people knew where he had gone, for some, both the righteous and the wicked, had seen him leave. Yet they were still hoping to find him.

"Maybe God has just taken Enoch away to one of his 'getaway spots,'" some suggested to each other. Those who loved Enoch looked very hard for him, just as someday the sons of the prophets would search for Elijah. But they didn't find him.

"Enoch 'is not,'" they came back and reported,

"for God has taken him."

By letting Enoch into heaven, God wanted to teach an important lesson. Because the results of sin are so dreadful there is a danger that we might become discouraged. Some who have tried to serve God might even say, "What's in it for us? Why should we respect God and try to keep His commandments, when there's such a heavy curse on the whole world, and we're all going to die anyway?"

But the teachings that God gave to Adam, handed down to Seth's children and lived out in Enoch's life, swept away the gloom and darkness and gave hope to the people. When they saw what happened to Enoch, they understood that even though death had come through Adam, life would come through Jesus, the promised Redeemer of the human race.

Satan wanted the people to believe there was no reward for doing right or punishment for doing wrong. He wanted people to think that it wasn't possible to obey God's law. But through the story of Enoch God showed that He will reward those who search after Him. It also told us what He will do for those who obey His commandments.

Through the example of Enoch, people can learn that it is possible to keep the law of God, even when sin surrounds them. With God's help they can resist temptation and become pure and holy. By looking at Enoch we can see how we may be blessed and even live forever by choosing to serve Jesus. We can also learn what will happen to those who decide not to follow Him.

The Bible tells us that "by faith Enoch was taken from this life, so that he did not experience death; he could not be found, because God had taken him away. For before he was taken, je was commended as one who pleased God" (Hebrews 11:5).

In the middle of a world that was so wicked God doomed it to destruction Enoch lived so close to God that the Lord would not permit him to die. Similarly, those people who are alive and waiting for Jesus to come at the end of time will have a character and closeness to God like Enoch did.

The level of holiness that he reached is an example of the holiness that we may have. Just before the Flood, wickedness appeared to be winning all over the world. And it will seem that way at the end of the world. People will follow their own hearts and rebel against God. But like Enoch, God's followers will look for purity of heart. They will obey His commandments and grow closer and closer to Him until they are more and more like Jesus. Like Enoch, the people living at the end of time will tell the world that Jesus is coming soon and warn about the judgment soon to fall on the wicked.

And like Enoch, God's people living in the end of the world will talk about holy things and live a holy life, and by doing so, condemn the sins of the wicked. God took Enoch to heaven just before He destroyed the world by water. Similarly, those who live at the end of time will be translated just before the Lord destroys the world by fire. The Bible says that "we will not all sleep, but we will all be changed—in a flash, in the twinkling of an eye, at the last trumpet. For the trumpet will sound, the dead will be raised imperishable, and we will be changed" (1 Corinthians 15:51, 52). "We who are still alive and are left will be caught up together with them in the clouds to meet the Lord in the air. And so we will be with the Lord forever. Therefore encourage each other with these words" (1 Thessalonians 4:17, 18).

CHAPTER • 13

Tripling the Curse

By the time Noah was born the earth suffered from a double curse. The first curse was for Adam's sin, and the second was for the murder committed by Cain. Yet in spite of the two curses, the earth was still beautiful. Towering trees loaded with fruit crowned the hills. Between the hills were vast, gardenlike valleys dressed in a living green and sweet with the fragrance of thousands of flowers.

The earth had many kinds of fruit—almost so many that you couldn't count them. As for the trees, they were much taller and more beautiful than any you can find today. The wood was different, too. It was hard like a rock and would almost last as long. Meanwhile, gold, silver, and beautiful gemstones littered the land.

In those days human beings were still extremely strong and healthy. Only a few generations had passed since Adam had been able to eat from the tree of life. When somebody asked, "How old are you?" people answered in centuries rather than in years.

If those powerful people, who could live so long and were so intelligent, had given themselves to serve and honor God, they would have made His name a praise in the earth. They would have done what He had in mind when He made them. But they didn't do this. Unfortunately, they were just as guilty as they were smart.

God gave these people who lived before the Flood many rich and wonderful gifts. But they used all of them to honor and praise themselves instead of Him. Turning His gifts into a curse instead of a blessing, they spent many years making beautiful homes for themselves. And they were always trying to outdo each other. It was like a contest to see who could build the fanciest house. Only concerned about themselves, they loved pleasure and wickedness.

They didn't want to think about God. Pretty soon, they even wanted to believe that He didn't exist. They loved nature more than the God who made it. Before long they worshiped the human mind and the things that it could make, and even taught their children to bow down to images. Out in the green fields, under the shadow of towering, majestic trees, they built many altars to their gods.

The beautiful gardens had long and winding paths through them. Fruit trees hung over the paths with scrumptious fruit of all kinds. Arches and arbors and probably even gazebos decorated the gardens. The people did everything they could think of in these gardens to delight their senses and make them feel happy. Ignoring God, they worshiped the things that they made. And because of this, they became more and more wicked.

In the Bible David the psalmist tells us what happens to people when they worship idols instead of God. "Those who make them will be like them," he says, "and so will all who trust in them" (Psalm 115:8).

It is a law of the human mind that what we look at changes us. People cannot rise any higher than their ideas of truth and purity and holiness. If the mind never goes above the human level, if it never looks up in faith to think about God and His infinite wisdom and love, it will sink lower and lower. And that's exactly what happened to the people who lived before the Flood.

They made their gods to be like sinful humans, and then they worshiped them. And so their standard of what to be like went lower and lower. As a result, they plunged deeper and deeper into sin.

God saw that human wickedness had become great in the earth. People thought only evil all the time. "The earth was corrupt in God's sight and was full of violence" (Genesis 6:11).

The Lord gave human beings His commandments as a rule to live by. But now they were stomping all over His law, doing every sin you could possibly think of. People became bolder and more daring in their sin. When they treated God's children unfairly, the cries of injustice went right to God's ears.

As sin crept into the human heart people did

whatever they wanted. Because of their selfish ways of living, crime and unhappiness rapidly filled the earth. Many of the wicked committed the sin of polygamy. The book of Genesis tells us that God gave Adam one wife. By doing that, God showed us the way He wanted things to be. He made marriage to be a sacred thing. But the people living before the Flood did not honor the gift of marriage.

Nor did they respect other people and their property. If a man wanted the wife or the land of his neighbor and he was stronger, he just went and took what he wanted. More than that, he bragged about what he had done. People began to love to kill animals, and the practice of meat-eating made them still more cruel and blood-thirsty. Soon they couldn't care less about whether even a human being lived or died.

The earth was still young. Yet sin had become so terrible that God couldn't stand it any longer. Extremely sad, He said, "I will wipe mankind, whom I have created, from the face of the earth" (Genesis 6:7). He decided that the Holy Spirit wouldn't always work with guilty humans. They would have to make a choice. And if they didn't decide to stop polluting the world with their sins, God, the great Creator, would actually destroy the things that He had delighted to make. He would sweep away the animals and all the greenery that made such an abundant supply of food in the earth. And He would turn this beautiful, magnificent earth into one vast scene of desolation and ruin.

CHAPTER • 14

Keepers of the Flame

In the midst of all this wickedness a group of people still worked to let others know about the true God. Individuals such as Methuselah and Noah tried to hold back the tide of evil. God also warned humanity what was going to happen. One hundred and twenty years before the Flood God sent an angel to tell Noah what He planned to do and to build an ark, or boat.

While he constructed the ark, Noah was to preach that God was going to bring a flood on the earth to destroy the wicked. If the people would heed Noah's message and get ready for the Flood by living holy lives, the Lord would forgive and save them.

God had

also told Enoch about the Flood, and Enoch told his children what would happen. Methusaleh and his sons, who lived long enough to hear Noah preach, helped to prepare the ark.

The Lord explained to Noah exactly how to build the ark. He even gave him the measurements. And as smart as humans were in those days, they could never have constructed such a strong and sturdy boat by themselves. But though God was the one who designed the ark, Noah was the one who made it. In some ways it looked like a ship, and in other ways it resembled a house. Three stories high, it only had one door, which was on the side.

The ark had a window at the top, and the different sections below were designed so that light could reach all of them. Noah used a special kind of wood in the ark, called cypress or gopher wood. It wouldn't rot for hundreds of years. Because of the wood's hardness, the work of building the ark took a long time.

Noah and his helpers did everything they could to make the ark perfect. But without God's help, it still couldn't have floated through the terrible storm that was about to strike the earth. Only God could preserve His servants through the height of that tempest. "By faith Noah, when warned about things not yet seen, in holy fear built an ark to save his family. By his faith he condemned the world and became heir of the righteousness that comes by faith" (Hebrews 11:7).

While Noah was preaching about the Flood that would soon devastate the world, the things he was doing showed that he really meant what he said. His building the ark demonstrated that he really believed

what he said. Noah spent everything he had on the ark. And as he began to build the huge boat, thousands of people came from every direction to see the strange sight. They wanted to hear the sincere words of this unusual preacher. Meanwhile, every hammer blow was a sermon in itself telling the people of what was soon to come.

At first, many people believed Noah's warning. But they didn't turn to God with all their hearts, because they didn't want to give up their sins. During the 120 years that passed between when Noah started to preach and when the Flood actually started, God tested the faith of the people. But, unfortunately, most of them failed to pass the test.

So many of the people around them didn't believe that those who did believe eventually left Noah. In their hearts many really believed the words of Noah, and they would have gone into the ark. But when others made fun of the ark and Noah's message, most of his followers gave up their belief. And those who had once believed became some of the boldest and most defiant scoffers.

It's sad to say, but nobody is so reckless or goes to such depths of sin as one who has seen God's light but chosen not to follow it.

In Noah's day many people were not idol worshippers in the fullest sense of the word. In fact, many claimed to worship God. They claimed that their idols could actually show them more about God. And sadly, such religious-minded people had the most to say against the preaching of Noah. As they tried to worship God through their idols, they became blind to the majesty of His power. Not realizing how holy

He really is, they became confused and didn't realize that His law doesn't change. So many people were sinning that sin didn't seem too bad. Finally, even many of the religious people said that God's law was no longer in force.

Because the Lord was a God of love, they thought He would never punish sinners. They didn't want to believe that God's judgments would ever fall on the earth. If the people of Noah's day had been obeying God's law, they would have recognized His voice in the warnings of His servant. But, unfortunately, their minds had become so blinded by rejecting the light that they really believed Noah's message was wrong.

Not many people now stood on the side of right. The whole world was against God's justice and His laws, and they thought of Noah as a strange or fanatical person.

The first lie Satan told Eve was "you will not surely die" (Genesis 3:4). And now, great and wise persons, honored by the world, were telling the same lie. "God is just trying to scare us into being good," they said. "He won't really punish the world. God is love, so He would never destroy the beautiful world He made or punish the beings He created.

"So don't worry," they told the people. "Noah is just a wild fanatic." The world joked about what a crazy old man Noah was. Instead of humbling their hearts before God, they sinned more and more. They acted as if the Lord hadn't said anything to them through His servant. Through all this trouble, Noah stood like a rock in the middle of a storm. Though everyone around him made fun of him, he still lived a holy life and was faithful to God. His preaching was powerful, too, because it was the voice of God speaking to humanity through His servant. Noah was a spiritually strong man because he was connected with God. For 120 years his solemn voice fell on the ears of the people, telling them that the Flood, which they thought was totally impossible, would someday come.

CHAPTER • 15

The Day Mercy Ended

In those days scientists thought that the laws of nature would always work in the same way. Spring, summer, fall, and winter had always come in their order. There had never been any type of flood up until that time, not even on the banks of a river. Instead, the rivers had always sent their waters safely to the sea.

The scientists who believed the laws of nature could never change didn't understand God's power. As the years went by and the people saw that nothing happened, even those who were afraid when Noah first started preaching began to feel reassured. Like many people today, they thought that nature was above the God of nature. They also assumed that nature's laws were so strong that God Himself couldn't change them.

"If what Noah says is right," they said, "nature would be turned out of its course. And that just can't happen." To their minds, Noah had to be wrong. They looked down on God's message with disgust and showed it by continuing to have parties and feasts at which they ate and drank way too much. They planted and built, bought and sold, and made plans for everything they would do in the future without even thinking about the Flood that would soon overtake the earth.

The people of Noah's time also believed that if there was any truth to what he said, the wisest people would understand it. If those of Noah's day had only been sorry for their sins and turned their lives around, God would not have brought the Flood.

When the people of Nineveh repented at the preaching of Jonah, God turned aside his anger. He would have done the same thing for the people before the Flood. But by being so stubbornly sinful and refusing to listen to Noah, God's prophet, they filled up the cup of their sinfulness and became ready for the destruction of the Flood. Their chance to turn around was nearly behind them.

Noah had done everything that God told him to do. The ark was built just as He said it should be. It was even filled with food for both people and animals. Then Noah gave his last solemn appeal to the people with an agony that can hardly be described. With tears, he begged them to enter the ark before it was too late.

Once again the people rejected his words. The crowd around the ark started shouting, making fun of him as a deluded old man. But suddenly silence fell on the mocking throng. Animals of every kind, from the fiercest to the most gentle, now began to come from the mountains and forest. Quietly they made their way toward the ark.

Then everyone heard a great rushing wind. Up in the air birds flocked from all directions. There were so many of them the sky became dark, and they flew in perfect order, straight into the ark! The animals obeyed God's command, while humans were disobedient. Holy angels guided the creatures two by two into the ark, while some animals that God set aside especially for offerings went in by sevens.

Amazed, the people called their scientists to explain what was going on. But the experts couldn't. It was a mystery they couldn't understand. Humanity had become so hardened by rejecting the warnings of God that even animals flocking from all over toward the ark made only a small impression. The people looked around them at the sun shining in its glory and at the earth still in almost Edenlike beauty. They pushed the fears out of their hearts by having yet a bigger party. Even worse, they kept on hurting and killing other people. It seemed as if they were daring or even inviting God to punish them.

Then God talked to Noah.

"You and your family come into the ark," He said, "for you are the only good person I have seen in your generation."

The whole world had rejected Noah's message. But his faithfulness had resulted in a blessing to his family. God rewarded him for his loyal service by saving all its members with him. What an encouragement this should be to parents today.

But outside the ark the time of mercy had ended. Noah and his family, the animals, and even the birds were inside the ark. "Then the Lord shut [them] in" (Genesis 7:16). A dazzling light, more vivid than lightning, dropped from the sky and hovered in front of the ark. Then the huge ark door, which was impossible for Noah and his family to close, slowly swung into place by unseen hands. Noah and his family were shut in, and those who rejected God's mercy were shut out.

The seal of heaven was on the door of the ark. God alone had shut it, and He alone could open it. It will also be this way again at the end of the world. There will come a day when Jesus will stop offering mercy to sinners. Before God comes in the clouds of heaven He will shut the door of mercy. No more will divine grace stop the wicked. Satan will have full control of sinners. Then those people who have rejected God will try to destroy His people. But just as God shut Noah in the ark, so He will then protect those who love and honor Him.

CHAPTER • 16

Satan Gets Wet

For seven days after Noah and his family went into the ark the world went on peacefully with no sign of the coming storm. Those seven days were a real test of their faith and a time of seeming triumph to the world outside. The fact that God delayed the Flood made the wicked think that Noah's message really was wrong and that the Flood would never come. The solemn things they had seen—the animals and birds going into the ark, the angel of God closing the door—they put out of their minds and continued to party. They thought all the miracles that God had just worked were just a big joke! And so a mob gathered around the ark, making fun of those inside with words more daring than they had ever used before.

But on the eighth day dark clouds filled

the sky. Soon the people heard murmurings of thunder and saw flashes of lightning. Large drops of rain began to fall. The world had never seen anything like this before, and the people were afraid. In their hearts they wondered whether Noah might have been right after all.

In the meantime, the sky became darker and darker while the rain came down faster and faster. The animals outside the ark were afraid and roamed around in the wildest terror. Their bellows and moos and caws seemed to cry out their own sad destiny and the fate of wicked humanity.

Then "all the springs of the great deep burst forth, and the floodgates of the heavens were opened" (Genesis 7:11). Water poured out of the clouds in huge torrents. Down below, rivers broke away from their banks and spilled over into the valleys. Jets of water exploded out of the ground with indescribable force, throwing massive rocks hundreds of feet into the air. When they fell, they buried themselves deep into the ground.

The storm first destroyed all the beautiful things the people had made. Lightning shattered all their buildings and the groves where they had put their idols. The tempest demolished the altars in which they had offered human sacrifices and scattered the ruins far and wide. And those who had conducted such wicked things trembled before the power of the living God.

The Lord wanted the people to know that it was their own corruption and idolatry that had led to their destruction. As the storm became more and more violent, it hurled trees, buildings, and rocks in every direction. Both people and animals were terrified beyond belief. Above the roar of the tempest one could hear the wailing of the people—people who had rebelled against divine authority.

God made Satan stay on the earth during the Flood. And because it was so terrible, even Satan was afraid and wondered if he would survive it. The devil had loved to control the powerful human race. He wanted them to live and to continue their rebellion against the ruler of heaven. Now he cursed God and blamed Him for being unkind and unfair.

Many of the people, like Satan, also cursed God. If they had been able, they would have torn Him from his very throne. Frantic with fear, they stretched their hands toward the ark and begged to be let in. Their consciences at last realized that there is a God who rules in the heavens. They cried to Him, but their pleas were in vain.

In that terrible, terrible hour, the people saw that they had caused their own ruin by breaking God's law. Even then, while they were afraid of their punishment and knew they had sinned, they weren't truly sorry for what they had done. They didn't really hate evil. If God had stopped the rain, they would have gone right back to their sinful ways.

When God's judgments fall on the earth at the end of the world, those who have hated God will understand that their sin has been in despising His holy law. But they won't be any sorrier for their sin than those who died in the Flood.

In their desperation some of the people tried to break into the ark. But the ship was so strongly made that they couldn't get in. Some held onto it until the surging waters washed them away. Or they lost their hold when the ark slammed into a rock or tree.

Even the massive ark, as strong as it was, trembled as the merciless waves pounded it. The animals inside the ark cried out in fear, but the ark rode safely.

Outside the ark animals rushed toward the people as if expecting humans to save them. Some of the people tied their children and themselves on these powerful animals, knowing that the creatures would fight for life and climb to the highest points to get away from the rising waters. Others tied themselves to the tops of the tallest trees on hills or mountains. But waves uprooted the trees and hurled them with their human cargo into the seething sea.

From the highest mountain peaks those few people who were still alive looked down on a shoreless ocean of water. No longer could they make fun of Noah's solemn warnings. How they wished they could have another chance to change their mind and board the ark. And they begged God for one more moment of mercy, one more call from the lips of Noah. But the voice of mercy would speak no more.

God's love, just as much as His justice, required that He put a stop to their terrible sin. And so the billowing waves swept over the last mountain peak, and those who hated God died in the depths of the ocean.

CHAPTER • 17

A Storm of Fire

The Bible tells us that, as it was in the days of Noah, another storm is yet to come. Once again God's wrath will sweep the earth clean. It will destroy sin and sinners. The same sins that brought down the wrath of God on the world before the Flood people repeat today. They still do not respect God and don't think much of His law, either.

Jesus Himself said that in the last days the world would be much as it was before Noah's flood. "For in the days before the flood, people were eating and drinking, marrying and giving in marriage, up to the day Noah entered the ark; and they knew nothing about what would happen until the flood came and took them all away. That is how it will be at the coming of the Son of Man" (Matthew 24:38, 39).

Now, there

is nothing wrong with eating and drinking. God gave the people before the Flood fruit in abundance to nourish their bodies. But they sinned by taking His gifts and not saying thank You to the one who gave them. In addition, they ate way too much without restraint. Nor is there anything wrong with people getting married. In fact, God designed marriage. The home was one of the first blessings that He ever gave to humanity.

God also gave people special directions about marriage. But people forgot them. Instead, they perverted marriage and used it in wrong ways.

Sins that took place before the Flood continue to happen today. Things that are OK in themselves get done out of order or way too much. People eat and drink without restraint. Even Christians, those who say they love and honor God, are eating and drinking with the drunken. Their names are on the church books, but all their overeating and gluttony numbs their ability to think. And this makes it easier for them to fall into all types of sin.

Many people assume that they are under no obligation to try to do what is right. They have become the slaves of sin, living for sensual pleasures in this world and this life alone. Extravagance, luxury, and display have swept the world. People seek to be rich while doing unfair things and making life hard for the poor. Stealing and bribery are rampant in all levels of society. The news is full of stories about murders and crimes so cold-blooded as to seem as if every element of human love has been blotted out.

The lack of love and compassion has become so common that people don't even think of them anymore. The threat of lawlessness is all over the world, and the civil wars that break out and the crimes are just the beginning of the many things that will happen before Christ returns. The way the world was before the Flood is very much the way the world is today. Even in countries that claim to be Christian, we find crimes committed daily that are as black and terrible as those for which God destroyed humanity by the Flood.

God sent Noah to warn the people, to try to save from destruction, to lead them back to Him. And during the last days before Christ's second coming God will once again have His servants prepare the world for that great day. Many people have been breaking God's law, living in sin, but in His great mercy He is calling them back to obey its sacred precepts. All who put away their sins and repent by believing in God and Jesus Christ will be forgiven. But many people think that God is asking them too much when He urges them to put away their sins.

Because the way they live doesn't fit with the pure principles of God's law and government, they reject His warnings and say that His law has no authority over them. Before Jesus, the one who gave the law, comes to punish those who disobey Him, He will have His servants ask sinners to give up their sins and return to God. But sadly, for many people, these warnings will be in vain.

Paul warns us that the world will become more and more wicked as the end of time draws near. "In later times," he wrote, "some will abandon the faith and follow deceiving spirits and things taught by demons" (1 Timothy 4:1).

Paul also says that in the last days perilous times shall come (2 Timothy 3:1). Then he gives a startling list of sins that will be found even among those who say they love God. Just before the Flood, when their time to choose to do what was right was almost up, the people threw more and more exciting parties and festivals. Leaders worked hard to keep the minds of the people occupied with mirth and pleasure. They didn't want anyone to listen to the solemn warning. The same thing is happening today.

God's people are trying to warn that the end of the world is near. But the people of the world are busy entertaining themselves. Constant excitement keeps them from paying attention to the truths of God's word—truths that alone can save them from the coming destruction.

When the wise men and women of Noah's time had convinced themselves that it was impossible for the world to be destroyed by a flood, when the people were afraid no longer, when everybody had decided that Noah's prophecy about a flood was a lie and thought he was crazy, that was the time for God to act. The fountains in the great deep then broke up and the windows of heaven opened (Genesis 7:11).

The proud scientists and thought leaders found out too late that all their wisdom was foolishness. That the God who gave the laws was greater than the laws themselves. And He has many ways to accomplish what needs to be done. As it was in the days of Noah, even thus shall it be in the day when the Son of Man returns (Luke 17:26-30). "The day of the Lord will come like a thief. The heavens will disappear with a roar; the elements will be destroyed by fire, and the earth and everything in it will be laid bare" (2 Peter 3:10).

Today, in the end of time, when the world is obsessed with business and pleasure, sudden destruction will strike it and none except God's people will escape it (1 Thessalonians 5:3).

CHAPTER • 18

God Makes a Promise

During the Flood the water rose above even the highest mountains. The storm was so fierce that Noah and his family in the ark often thought they would die. For five long months the boat, at the mercy of the winds and the waves, tossed on the worldwide sea.

It was a difficult time for Noah and his family. But his faith didn't waver. He knew that God's hand was guiding the ship. As the flood water began to go down, God guided the ark into the shelter of a cluster of mountains that He had protected during the Flood. There the ark floated more quietly in this quiet haven. No longer did the high waves drive it across the boundless ocean. It made life easier for the ship's exhausted passengers.

Noah and his family were tired of being on the boat. They could hardly wait to get out and walk on solid ground again. Forty days after they could see the tops of the mountains through the windows of the ark, they decided to send out a raven to see if the rest of the land was getting dry or not. If there was dry land out there, they thought, the bird would find it. But the raven saw nothing but water as it flew back and forth from the ark.

Seven days later Noah released a dove. But like the raven, the dove returned to the ark. Noah didn't give up, however. After another seven days he released a second dove. When the dove returned that night with an olive leaf in its mouth, Noah and his family were very happy.

The top of the ark had a covering that Noah could take off. When he did so, he and his family could see that the ground was dry. But as eager as they were to leave the ark, they still waited inside. They had gone into the ark when God told them too. Now they waited for His direction to leave.

Then one wonderful day an angel came down from heaven and opened the massive door of the ark. "You may come out of the ark," the angel told them. "And take all the birds and animals with you." Even in his joy to be out of the ark, Noah didn't forget to say thank You to God for keeping him safe. And so the first thing he did after leaving the ark was to build an altar. There he made an offering to God, taking one of every kind of clean animal.

By doing this he thanked God for saving them. He

was also showing his belief in Jesus, who would one day die for his sins. God was pleased with Noah's offering. And so He blessed Noah's family, and not only them, but everyone who would one day live on the earth. God said in His heart, "Never again will I curse the ground because of man, even though every inclination of his heart is evil from childhood. And never again will I destroy all living creatures, as I have done. As long as the earth endures, seedtime and harvest, cold and heat, summer and winter, day and night will never cease" (Genesis 8:21, 22).

We find an important lesson for us in the story of Noah. When he left the ark the earth was barren and desolate. But before he made a house for himself, he built an altar to God. Noah didn't have a lot of animals, and it had cost him a lot of time and effort to save the ones he had. Yet he cheerfully sacrificed part of everything he had to God.

By this he showed that he understood that everything he owned really belonged to God. We should thank God for all the wonderful things He does for us and show Him that we love Him—both by the things we do and the gifts we give to His cause.

Because of what had happened at the Flood God knew that people might be filled with terror every time clouds gathered or rain began to fall. But because of Noah's thankfulness and sacrifice, the Lord gave him, his family, and everyone to follow a special promise.

"I will establish My covenant with you," He said. "Never again will there be another Flood to destroy the earth. I will set My bow in the cloud, and it will be a token of the covenant between Me and the earth. From now on when I bring a cloud over the earth, that bow

will appear in the cloud, and as I look at it, I will remember the everlasting covenant between Me and every living creature." (See Genesis 9:8-17.)

So anytime you see a rainbow in the sky, it is a promise that not only will God not send another Flood, but that He loves you very much. So during the centuries to come, whenever children would see the rainbow arching across the sky after a rain, and they asked their parents what it meant, God wanted the parents to tell the story of the Flood. That the God who put it in the clouds had promised that He would never again destroy the whole earth by a flood.

CHAPTER • 19

Three Sons, Three Directions

Things must have looked pretty bleak to Shem, Ham, and Japheth during those first few days out of the ark. They had seen the exquisite gardens, magnificent palaces, and well-planned cities that existed before the Flood. More than that, they had worshiped at the gates of the most beautiful garden of all—the forbidden Garden of Eden.

But now the land was a desolate, mud-covered wasteland. And it was their job, as sons of the only family saved from the fateful Flood, to rebuild the earth and fill it with their own sons, daughters, and grandchildren.

It must have seemed like a monumental

task to them at first. Having been spared by believing God's message to their father, Noah's three strapping sons probably had quite a bit of faith that they could do it.

And they had good intentions, too, as they trooped down the gangplank of the ark with their wives and a thousand braying, bleating, and mooing animals. But, unfortunately, good intentions don't always translate into wise choices. Each of Noah's children already had seeds of sin growing together with the good seeds. And the three sons would pass their heritage of good or bad on to their children, depending, of course, on which seeds they watered and allowed to grow in their hearts.

Noah understood this, of course. For he was not only the great-great-grandaddy of us all, he was also a prophet. And so God spoke through Noah, telling the direction each of his three sons and their descendants would take. And, unfortunately, Noah saw a pretty harsh future for the children of Ham, his youngest son.

"Cursed be Canaan," said Noah, speaking of Ham's son. "He will be a servant of servants to his brothers." In contrast, the future looked brighter for the children of Shem and Japheth.

"Blessed be the Lord, the God of Shem," Noah went on. "And Canaan shall be his servant. God will extend the territory of Japheth, and he will dwell in Shem's tents. Canaan will also be his servant."

Of course, there was a reason for the things God predicted through Noah. The predictions were not arbitrary. Shem, Ham, and Japheth were already making choices that would affect not only their lives, but the direction their children would take. Not too long after the Flood Ham had already been horribly disrespectful to his father. More than that, he showed by his words and actions that he had not respected Noah for a long time.

Perhaps some of those wild accusations made against Noah before the Flood got under Ham's skin. In spite of the fact that the faith of his father had saved Ham from the Flood, he treated the old man with contempt. More than that, he passed the evil traits of character he was developing on to his children and grandchildren.

That is why Ham's punishment was actually passed on to his son. Although it didn't have to be that way, God saw far in advance what the children of Ham would be like. And because of their sins, they would be punished with the curse of slavery.

Shem and Japheth, on the other hand, were making a better set of choices. The line of Shem would be especially important. One of Shem's great-great-very-great grandchildren would be none other than Jesus Christ Himself. In addition, the family of Shem would include many Bible characters who loved and served God, such as Abraham and Sarah, Isaac and Rebekah, Moses, David, and Daniel. While the children of Japheth didn't have quite the future to look forward to that the children of Shem did, God promised that they would "live in the tents of Shem" (Genesis 9:27). By this God meant that they would share in the blessings of the gospel message along with the children of Shem.

Of course, none of these things had to happen. God did not fix the character of Shem, Ham, and

Japheth. He only saw in advance what would be the sad and/or happy results of the direction their feet were already heading.

Because children often grow up to be like their parents, the choices made by these three sons were especially important. They would be passing on something very important—either their good or bad traits of character—to their children for years and years and years to come.

The Bible says that "one sinner destroys much good" (Ecclesiastes 9:18). In contrast, one righteous person can encourage many good things.

"The Lord knoweth the days of the upright" (Psalm 37:18, KJV) "and his seed is blessed" (Psalm 37: 26, KJV). "Know therefore that the Lord your God is God; he is the faithful God, keeping his covenant of love to a thousand generations of those who love him and keep his commands" (Deuteronomy 7:9).

Shem showed by his actions that he greatly respected both his father and God. He passed on this attitude of respect to his children, and as a result, an impressive line of holy men and women were born and raised in his family.

CHAPTER • 20

Building on Wrong Ideas

You would think that, after the horrors of the Flood, no one would soon forget its lessons. We can be sure that Shem, Ham, and Japheth told their children all about it, for many cultures of the world have deep in their pasts preserved the history of a worldwide Flood. But though human beings have long remembered the Flood, when it comes to the lessons to learn from it, it seems that they have very short memories. Within 100 years of the Flood—even while Noah was still alive—people were right back at their wicked ways again.

The problem seemed to begin with a set of wrong ideas. In the previous chapter, we mentioned that Noah's son, Ham, showed a terrible lack of respect for his father. This is very serious, for too often, a lack of respect for earthly parents becomes a lack of respect for God.

Ham passed his attitude of disrespect on to his offspring, and many of Shem and Japheth's children must have joined in on it, too, for a lot of the people of that time banded together to come up with a bad idea.

Of course, some still continued to follow God. But just as they had before the Flood, the followers of God were a thorn in the flesh to those who wanted to forget about their Creator. This time it was those who rejected God who decided to move away.

They picked a beautiful spot for themselves on the plain of Shinar along the banks of the Euphrates River. The area had an abundance of fertile soil for growing food, and there the people decided to make their home.

Although God had told the people to scatter all over the earth, the people of Shinar wanted to stay together. So they decided to build a city, which they hoped would eventually grow into a strong enough kingdom to rule the entire world. The city would be grand and glorious, making its builders famous in other lands. In the center of the city would be an incredible tower, which would stand not only as a monument to the power and wisdom of its builders, but save them from any future floods.

Of course, that was the problem. God had promised not to bring another worldwide flood on the earth. But by building a massive tower the people showed their lack of faith in God's promise. More than that, some of them didn't even think God was real. Others decided the Flood was only a fluke of nature.

And still others believed in God, but like Cain, were angry with Him for destroying the world.

And so they built their incredible tower up toward the clouds, hoping that when they got there, they would even be able to find out what caused the Flood. It was quite a project, requiring much planning and lots of building materials. The people of that day were still much stronger and more intelligent than humans today, so we can only imagine that they could build a bigger and stronger skyscraper than any that New York, Chicago, or San Francisco has ever seen.

As the tower rose higher and higher, it became necessary to station people on the different levels. The worker at the top would call down to the fellow just below, and so on until the requests for more bricks, beams, or other building supplies reached the bottom.

When the people weren't busy working, they often passed the time by murmuring against God. Many of them felt that He had been too hard on Adam, then Cain, and then the people before the Flood. But while they turned away from God as a tyrant, they didn't realize that they were beginning to serve Satan—the cruelest tyrant of all. Soon hatred toward God replaced the love they had once had in their hearts. As they turned farther and farther from God, they even began to offer their own children as human sacrifices.

During this time some who believed in God were tricked into working on the tower. Because they didn't understand what was going on, the Lord let things continue until they could understand. Others who loved and honored God, however, saw clearly the danger of the Tower of Babel. As they watched the wicked people setting up their mighty kingdom, with which they hoped to forever banish everything good and right from the earth, the good people begged God to stop the great tide of wickedness that seemed poised to sweep the world once again.

Of course, God's ears are always open to the cry of His people. And while He is committed to fighting fair in the war with Satan, to letting evil take its course so that all can be sure where it leads, there are also limits to what He allows. Although some may have been confused, God understood exactly what was happening on the plain of Shinar. Here was a kingdom built on pride, founded in rebellion, thriving on defiance, and increasingly committed to banishing peace and justice from the face of the earth. The God of the universe, though very patient, had seen enough.

The tower was fast filling up with luxurious balcony-view apartments, set aside to honor the builders. It also had rooms for idols, splendidly furnished with the best that money could buy. Elated at their success, the people praised their gods of gold and silver for helping them build the tower. It was then—at that moment in the history of the tower—that "the Lord came down to see the city and the tower that the men were building" (Genesis 11:5).

CHAPTER • 21

The Tower Comes Tumbling Down

Bring me 500 bricks!" someone shouted at the top of the tower.

"Bring me 500 bricks!" the second person in the relay repeated.

"Bring me 500 bricks!" rang the voice of the individual on each level until the message reached the bottom.

It was the method they had used to order more material since the tower first reached into the sky, and it worked very well. Until one day, that is.

Evidently they didn't realize that a very important building inspector had visited their site. It was God, of course. And, like a lot of other building inspectors, He didn't like what He saw.

Now if your local building inspector doesn't think you did something right, he or she normally asks you to change it. But in this case the inspector wasn't concerned with "how" the tower was built. He knew it should never have been constructed at all. And so He decided to take action—of the type that only a heavenly official can.

"Bring me 500 bricks!" ordered the person at the top of the tower.

"Bring me 25 sticks!" the second in the relay said.

"Bring me 84 hicks!" the third declared. And so the message changed at each level until it reached the bottom of the tower.

"Nine hundred hammers! What in the world do they want those for?" After a mad scramble, the materials foreman somehow located the goods and started them on their long, arduous trip to the top. Then come a set of other strange orders. It seemed that they wanted 6,000 garden hoes followed by 39 lemons and 12,000 oxen. Bring the oxen fast and the lemons slow, came the command, and get it all there in 10 minutes or less.

"What in the world is going on up there?" the materials supervisor shouted to the worker above him. Once more a message got relayed umpteen times until it reached the person at the top. But he was in no mood to answer, for the first installment of garden hoes had just arrived.

"What in the world is going on down there?" he demanded of the man below him just as a runner puffed up the steps with 39 lemons. Of course, it wasn't what was going on at the top or bottom of the tower that

mattered so much. It was the action high above it that stopped the construction. The God of heaven, who had taken time to personally visit this incredibly massive skyscraper, had decided to cancel the project.

He didn't bother sending them a notice, either, since they wouldn't have listened anyway. In spite of His best and most powerful efforts, communication with His stubborn children had broken down some time ago. And so now He did something that only God can do: He made it so that everybody now had a different language.

Perhaps the man at the top spoke Sumerian, the person below had become an Egyptian, he was above an Akkadian, and so on it went on down the line. With all the confusion, it didn't take long for tempers to flare. Soon shouting and cursing and violence broke out on nearly every level of the tower. Perhaps those at the top started raining down bricks, while the those at the bottom sent up 1,200 speedy soldiers instead of oxen. We don't know the exact details, but we do know that work on the tower came to a grinding and final halt. Not because the people wanted to stop, but because they could do nothing else.

And that is what always happens when people set themselves against God. Though God in His great kindness had allowed sin to go on for a while so that all might see where it led to, the natural result of sin is sadness, confusion, and death.

Because they were fighting against God and trying to stamp out His truth, the best-laid plans of the Babel builders ended in shame and defeat. Their giant tower—the monument to their pride and greatness—became instead the memorial of their sin and foolishness.

You would think we would all take a lesson from the grand old stories in the Bible. Yet many are still busy putting up their own incredible towers today. People who don't believe in God construct a set of false theories, while rejecting the plain truth that God has given in His Holy Word. Jeering at the principles of God's government, they hate His law and brag about how smart they are. Then, "when the sentence for a crime is not quickly carried out, the hearts of the people are filled with schemes to do wrong" (Ecclesiastes 8:11).

Sad to say, some of these tower builders even call themselves Christians. Yet they turn away from the simple teachings of the Bible and build their own creed, based on human guesses and ideas. Such people are proud of their towers, pointing to them in awe as they climb higher and higher, trying to reach into heaven. Others get confused by these towering lies, and come to believe such fables as the idea that sinners will not really die, or that people can be saved without learning to obey God.

The Bible defines the word "Babel" or "Babylon" as meaning "confusion," and there couldn't have been a more fitting name for that ancient, human-made edifice than "Tower of Confusion." Interestingly enough, the Bible also speaks of the world-loving churches at the end of time—those that have left the pure, simple word of the Bible—as "Babylon" or confusion. This is why there are so many churches. Instead of following the clear word of God, many are building their own personal towers.

But the God of heaven sees all that they do. No doubt He has visited the churches, as He did so long ago at the Tower of Babel. Because He knew people would use it to cause wickedness in the earth, God stopped the work on the Tower of Babel. More than that, by changing their language He forced them to spread throughout the earth. It was sad that this had to happen, for it would have been much easier to present the gospel without having to translate from one language to another. But given the rebellion and stubborn actions of Babel's builders, it was the best He could do.

Today, God is once again checking up on the people of this world. He is watching to see what they are building. He will show His power in these last days, and as He struck the Tower of Babel with a bolt of lightning, He will also demolish the works of human pride today.

FAMILY BIBLE STORY SERIES

One of the most extensively researched Bible story books on the market today, this series offers features which give background information to engage every member of the family, young and old alike. Written by Ruth Redding Brand and illustrated by distinguished artists, these carefully researched and beautifully illustrated books will make Bible characters come alive for your children. Every name, place, and custom is carefully explained. Hardcover. Available individually or as a set.

Abraham, 109 pages. ISBN 0-8280-1856-1

Adam & Eve, 95 pages. ISBN 0-8280-1850-2

Jacob, 127 pages. ISBN 0-8280-1852-9

Joseph, 87 pages. ISBN 0-8280-1854-5

Quick order online at www.AdventistBookCenter.com
Call 1-800-765-6955
Visit your local Adventist Book Center®
Or ask for it wherever books are sold